THE ULTIMATE BEGINNER SERIES®

BASS COMPLETE

Dale Titus • Roscoe Beck • Tim Bogart • Albert Nigro

Alfred Publishing Co., Inc.
16320 Roscoe Blvd., Suite 100
P.O. Box 10003
Van Nuys, CA 91410-0003
alfred.com

Book and DVD (with case)
ISBN-10: 0-7390-5614-X
ISBN-13: 978-0-7390-5614-1

Book and DVD (without case)
ISBN-10: 0-7390-5615-8
ISBN-13: 978-0-7390-5615-8

Cover photographs:
Blue energy © istockphoto.com/Raycat
Bass courtesy of Fender Musical Instruments Corporation

CONTENTS

BLUES BASS

ROCK BASS

CONTENTS

INTRODUCTION

The bass: it's such a fun and versatile instrument to play. As a member of the rhythm section, the bass helps to drive the band and define the harmony for the song, but it can also step into the spotlight and take a solo, or even play the melody. This book and DVD covers everything you'll need to start your journey toward mastering the bass and playing blues and rock.

The Basics section gets you started by teaching the various parts of the bass, how to tune and change strings, how to develop good picking and fretting techniques, great exercises that will develop strength and dexterity in both hands, and how to create and play some common bass lines. This section also provides some helpful tips on how to practice.

The Blues section will supply you with enough material to sound and play like greats such as Muddy Waters, Elmore James, Howlin' Wold, Albert King, B.B. King, and more. You'll explore topics like shuffles, slow blues, minor blues, and the two-beat feel. There is also an examination of right- and left-hand techniques.

The Rock section will show you some classic rock grooves and bass lines that every rock bass player needs to know, various right- and left-hand techniques, quarter-, eighth-, and sixteenth-note feels, how to work rhythmically with a drummer, and some special techniques such as harmonics, tapping, and double stops.

Also included are play-along tracks that will enable you to apply the new rhythms, techniques, and licks to music.

Let's dig in and get started playing bass.

The included DVD contains MP3 audio files of every example in the book. Use the MP3s to ensure you're capturing the feel of the examples and interpreting the rhythms correctly.

To access the MP3s on the DVD, place the DVD in your computer's DVD-ROM drive. In Windows, double-click on My Computer, then right-click on the DVD drive icon. Select Explore, then double-click on the DVD-ROM Materials folder. For Mac, double-click on the DVD icon on your desktop, then double-click on the DVD-ROM Materials folder.

BASIC BASS

TYPES OF BASSES

4-String

This is a four-string fretted bass. The four-string is the most commonly played bass today. Because of its simple design and versatility, the four-string bass is a great instrument for beginners.

Photo courtesy of Schecter Guitar Research

Photo courtesy of Meghan Joyce

Fretless Bass

This is a fretless bass. Because it has no frets on the fingerboard the fretless has a very distinctive sound. The fretless bass is also much harder to play so it is not recommended for beginners. If you happen to have a fretless, the information in this book will still be useful to you.

Photo courtesy of Schecter Guitar Research

Photo courtesy of Schecter Guitar Research

5- and 6-String Basses

The five- and six-string basses are relatively new to the public, but are quickly gaining popularity. The extra strings allow players to cover a wider range of pitches. Because of their wider necks and higher selling prices, most five- and six-string basses are not recommended for someone who's just starting out.

Strings

Bass strings are available in three basic gauges: light (soft), medium and heavy. Start with a light to medium gauge set of strings. An approximate starting gauge is .040 for the G string, .060 for the D string, .075 – .080 for the A string and .095 – .100 for the E string.

PARTS OF THE BASS

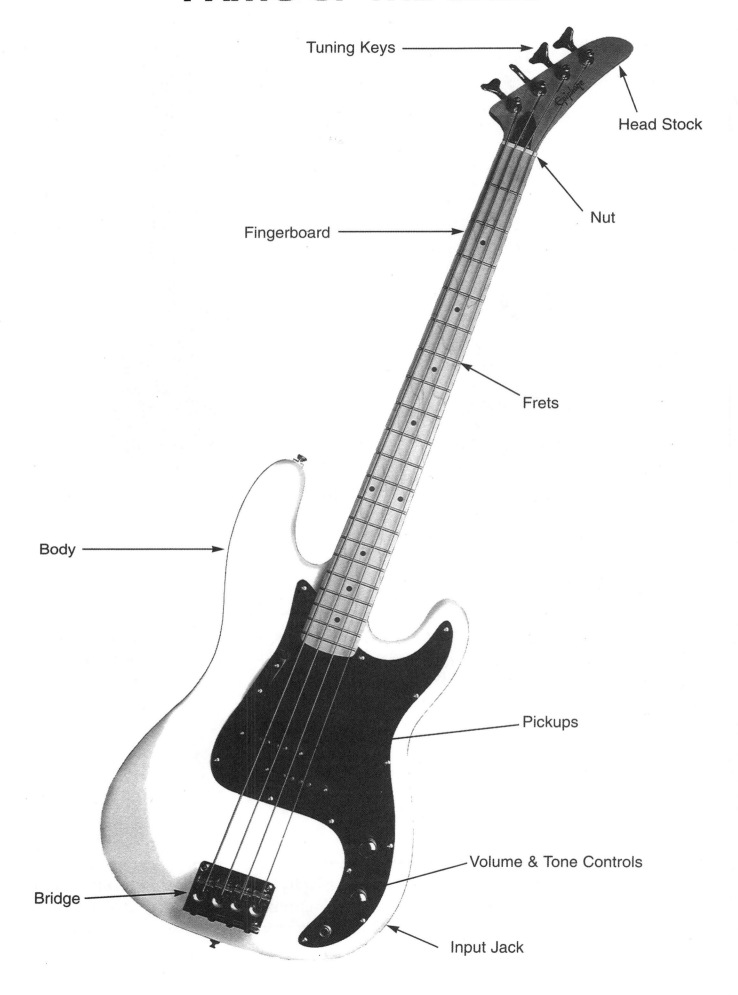

Tuning Keys

Head Stock

Nut

Fingerboard

Frets

Body

Pickups

Volume & Tone Controls

Bridge

Input Jack

Warwick rack mount system

AMPLIFIERS

When you're first starting out, look for an amplifier that's reliable, has a good size speaker and has the most power that you can afford to buy. Power is not for volume, it's for clarity, and it is important to get as much as you can. If you have no idea where to start, go to your bass instructor or ask a trusted friend that plays bass. Then, go down to a music store and play everything they have, ask questions and make an informed decision.

10

HOW TO TUNE UP

Electric Tuners:

Many brands of small, battery operated tuners, similar to the one shown below, are available. Simply follow the instructions supplied with your tuner.

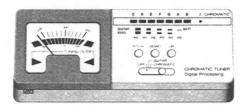

Tuning to a Piano or Electronic Keyboard:

An easy way to tune a bass is to a piano keyboard. The four strings of the bass are tuned to the keyboard notes shown in the following diagram.

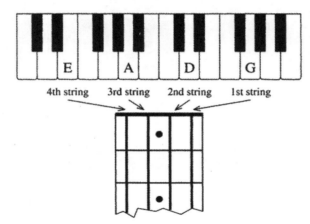

Tuning the Bass to Itself (Relative Tuning):

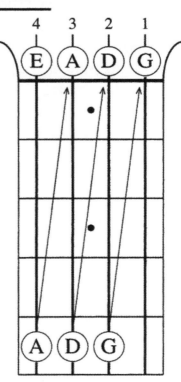

1. Tune the 1st string to G on the piano (or some other fixed pitch instrument, such as a pitch pipe).

2. Depress the 2nd string at the 5th fret. Play it and you will hear the note G, the same as the 1st string open. Turn the 2nd string tuning key until the pitch of the 2nd string matches of that of the 1st string.

3. Depress the 3rd string at the 5th fret. Play it and you will hear the note D, the same as the 2nd string open. Turn the 3rd string tuning key until the pitch of the 3rd string matches that of the 2nd string.

4. Depress the 4th string at the 5th fret. Play it and you will hear the note A, the same as the 3rd string open. Turn the 4th string tuning key until the pitch of the 4th string matches that of the 3rd string.

Tuning by Harmonics:

Another method of tuning is the harmonic method, which is a little more accurate because the tone is very pure and higher in pitch, making it easier to hear when the notes are in tune than using open strings. To play a harmonic on the bass, lightly touch the string directly over a fret (do not depress the string to the fretboard). Pluck with the picking hand. You should hear a ringing "bell" like sound.

To tune using harmonics:

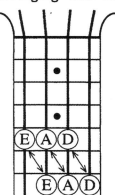

1. Play the harmonic on the fifth fret of the E string. This should match the harmonic on the seventh fret of the A string.

2. Once those strings are in tune, match the harmonic on the fifth fret of the A string to that on the seventh fret of the D string.

3. Finally, repeat this using the harmonics on the fifth fret of the D string and the seventh fret of the G string.

Listen for the waves to slow down and eventually stop when the strings are in tune. This method can also be used with electronic tuners. If the tuner doesn't respond well to the open strings, try using the harmonics at the twelfth fret of each string instead. The higher pitch and clearer tone usually provide a better signal from the instrument to the tuner.

CHANGING STRINGS

There are a few reasons you may have to change your strings: one, of course, is if you break a string; but strings will become dull sounding and harder to tune the longer you play them, so eventually they'll have to be replaced.

To replace a string:

1. Remove the old string. Do not remove all the old strings from your bass at once because this releases too much tension, which is bad for the neck. It is safer to remove only one string at a time. Also, it is better to loosen the strings with the tuning keys rather than cut them with wire cutters. Save the old strings as spares in case a new one breaks.

2. After the old string has been removed the new string is seated to the bridge; that is, the ball end is placed through the tailpiece and over the saddles of the bridge. On some models, the string must be pulled through the tailpiece. Be careful to put the correct string in the correct place as the different strings each have a different tension.

3. Stretch the string along the fingerboard, insert it into the proper tuning key and tighten either by hand or with a peg winder, keeping tension on the string and making sure each winding around the post is towards the head stock, not the tip of the post.

On models with a split tuning key, a small amount of excess string should be cut off the tip to allow proper fit on the post, generally 2-1/2 to 3 inches above the tuning key post. Insert the tip of the string into the hole and bend the string into the slot on the post.

The strings should wind to the outside of the post, and each string has a specific slot in the nut to seat in. After changing the string there will be a period in which the string will stretch. This can be hastened by pulling on the string or simply by playing.

NOTE NAMES ON THE FINGERBOARD

It's vital to know where all the notes are located on the bass. This will make jamming with other musicians much easier. It has been said that there is no real money above the fifth fret; although that is meant as a joke, a bass payer can do a lot of playing within the first five frets. Most of the exercises in this book stay within the first five frets.

The Musical Alphabet

The musical alphabet is made up of seven natural notes, named for the first seven letters of the alphabet (A - G). After G, we begin again with A. All notes are separated by a whole step, except for the notes E - F and B - C, which are separated by a half step. On the bass, a half step is equal to one fret and a whole step is equal to two frets.

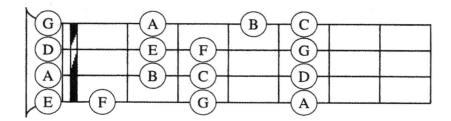

The notes in between the natural notes have names relating to them. For instance, the note between F and G is called either F sharp (indicated by the ♯ sign) or G flat (indicated by the ♭ sign), depending on the direction the notes are heading. Sharps raise the note a half step (up one fret) and flats lower the note a half step (down one fret).

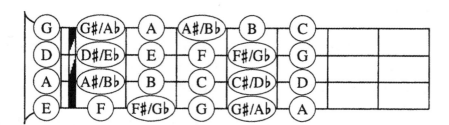

As shown in the tuning section, a note or pitch can be found in more than one location on the neck. Practice locating the same note on more than one string.

MUSIC NOTATION

The rhythms and note names are indicated by the standard notation, and the location of those notes on the neck of the bass is indicated by the tablature. Here are some basic rules of standard notation:

Music is written on a staff, which consists of five lines and four spaces (between the lines):

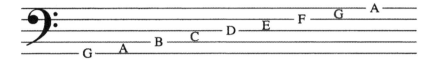

At the beginning of the staff is a bass clef (or F clef). The bass clef is used for all bass instruments.

The notes are written on the staff in alphabetical order. The first line is G:

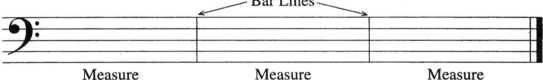

The staff is divided into *measures* by *bar lines*. A heavy double bar line marks the end of the music:

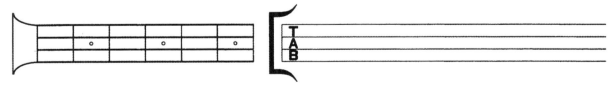

Tablature

Tablature is commonly used in conjunction with standard music notation. Tablature illustrates the location of notes on the neck of the bass. This illustration compares the four strings of a bass to the four lines of tablature.

Notes are indicated by placing fret numbers on the strings. An "O" indicates an open string.

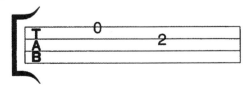

This tablature indicates to play the open, 1st, and 3rd frets on the 1st string.

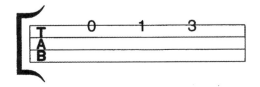

RHYTHM NOTATION AND TIME SIGNATURES

At the beginning of every song is a time signature. 4/4 is the most common time signature:

4 Four counts to a measure
4 A Quarter note receives one count

The top number tells how many counts per measure, the bottom number tells which kind of note receives one count.

The time value is determined by three things:

1) note head:

2) stem:

3) flag:

o This is a whole note. The note head is open and has no stem.
In 4/4 time, a whole note receives 4 counts.

This is a half note. It has an open note head and a stem.
A half note receives 2 counts.

This is a quarter note. It has a solid note head and a stem.
A quarter note receives 1 count.

This is an eighth note. It has a solid note head and a stem with a flag attached.
An eighth note receives 1/2 count.

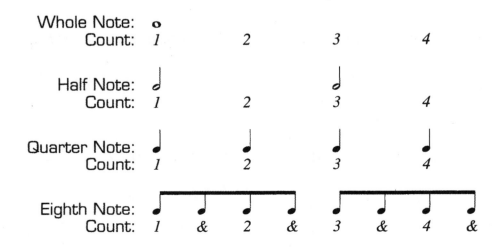

Whole Note:	o			
Count:	1	2	3	4
Half Note:				
Count:	1	2	3	4
Quarter Note:				
Count:	1	2	3	4
Eighth Note:				
Count:	1 &	2 &	3 &	4 &

PICKING AND RIGHT HAND TECHNIQUES

There are basically two ways to pluck the string: one is to use an actual pick, and the other is to play with two fingers of the right hand: the index and middle fingers. The pick gives a brighter sound with more attack and can be manipulated easier at faster tempos. The two-finger method, is the most common, producing a warm and distictive sound. When using this method, anchor your thumb to the bass, usually to the pickup. It is also important to alternate the right hand attack, either by picking down and up with the pick [indicated ⊓ and ∨] or alternating the index and middle fingers [indicated *i* and *m*].

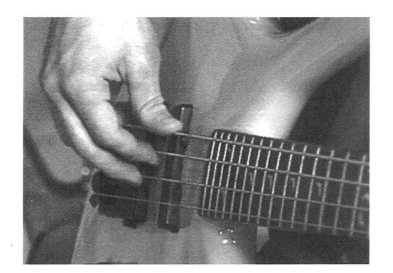 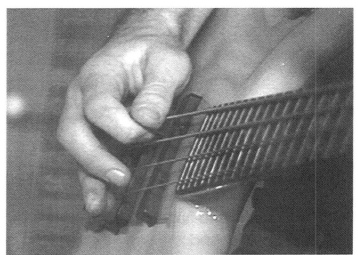

Example 1: Open String Exercise

This exercise concentrates on the right hand exclusively. Mute the strings with your left hand by gently holding the strings without actually fretting them. Remember to alternate the picking in the right hand.

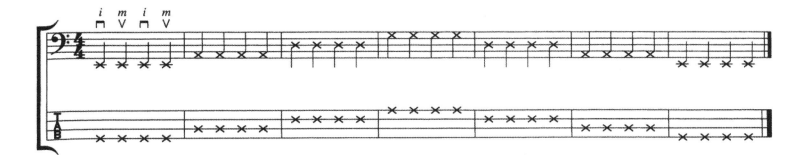

FRETTING TECHNIQUES

Once some coordination is established with the right hand, it is time to move on to the left hand, developing some basic fretting techniques. There are a few rules to keep in mind while practicing:

1) Keep the thumb on the back of the neck.

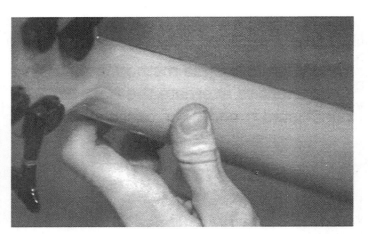

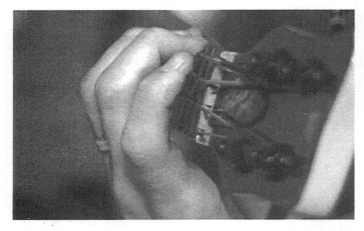

2) Play right behind, not on, the fret whenever possible.

3) Try to keep a one-finger-per-fret spacing with your left hand.

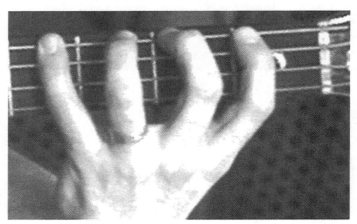

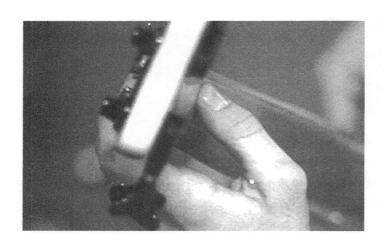

4) Leave a space between the palm of the left hand and the neck, not gripping too tightly.

Example 2: Fingerboard Exercise

This simple exercise helps to develop good, clean fretting technique. While doing this exercise, make sure to alternate the right hand fingers (or pick) consistently.

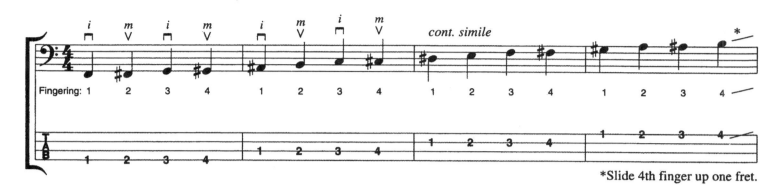

*Slide 4th finger up one fret.

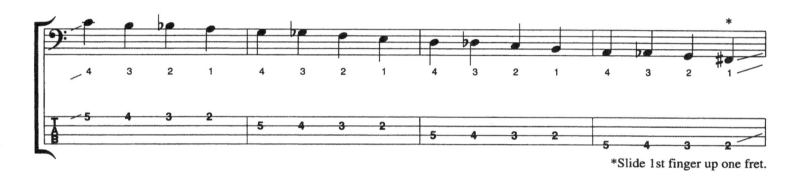

*Slide 1st finger up one fret.

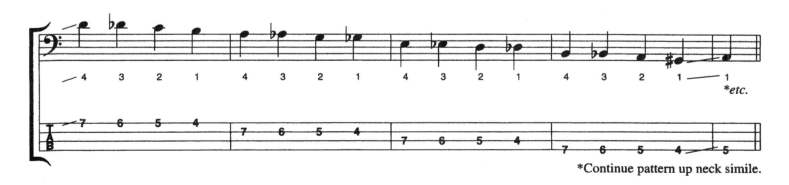

*Continue pattern up neck simile.

This is also a great exercise to develop technique up and down the neck of the bass. Spend about five minutes each day going through it to develop strong, consistent technique.

TIME TO PLAY

Common Bass Lines

Let's talk about how to create some common bass lines. First of all, in many musical situations the one note the bass player plays the most is the root of whatever chord is being played at the time. The root, or tonic, of a chord is the note on which the chord is built, and is where the chord gets its name. (The root of a C chord is C.)

Occasionally, the bass player wants to play some other notes to add some color to their bass lines, so they turn to other chord tones besides the root, or arpeggios, to find which notes to use. An arpeggio is made up from the notes of a chord played one at a time. Let's start with the arpeggio of a very common chord type: the major chord.

The Major Chord

The notes of a major arpeggio are the root, the third and the fifth. The third of a C major chord is three notes up the C major scale (C - D - E) and the fifth is five notes up the C major scale (C - D - E - F - G).

C Major Scale:	C	D	E	F	G	A	B	C
	1	2	3	4	5	6	7	8
C Major Chord:	C		E		G		
	1		3		5		

An easy way to play the major arpeggio is to play the root with the 2nd finger of the fretting hand. That makes the third easily reachable using the 1st finger, and the 4th finger can easily grab the fifth. This is great because you can move this arpeggio around just by knowing the root of the chord you're playing against. Practice this arpeggio pattern over C and then transpose it to G and D.

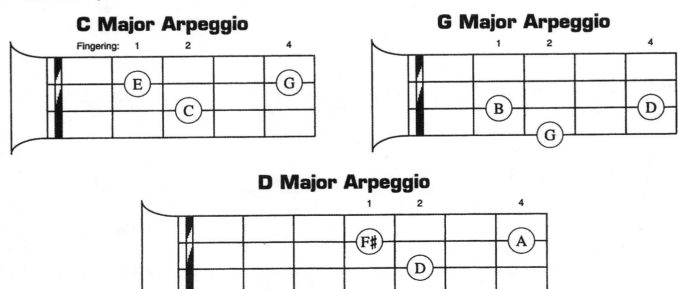

Example 3: G, C and D — Major Arpeggios

This example demonstrates three ways of creating a bass line using the major arpeggio with the roots G, C, and D. First, it gives just the root of each chord (Ex. 3A), then the straight arpeggio (Ex. 3B), next a little rhythmic variation that is similar to a common blues bass line (Ex. 3C) and finally a combination of these techniques (Ex. 3D). Play along with the rhythm track provided.

Example 3A — Root only

Example 3B — Major Arpeggio

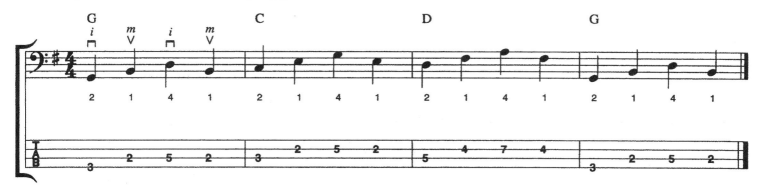

Example 3C — Rhythmic Variation

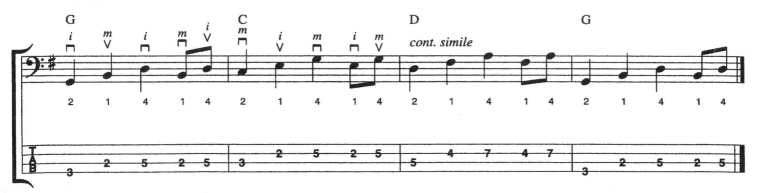

Example 3D — Compilation

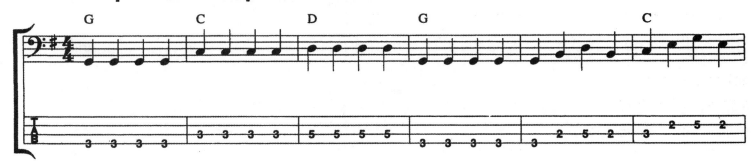

If while playing along you find it hard keeping up with the track, practice the patterns more slowly, until they become comfortable. It is important to always use a metronome or drum machine to maintain consistent time.

The Minor Chord

The minor chord is different than the major chord. The minor chord consists of the root, the flat third (a half step below the major chord third) and the fifth.

C Major Scale:	C	D	E	F	G	A	B	C
	1	2	3	4	5	6	7	8
C Major Chord:	C		E		G			
	1		3		5			
C Minor Chord:	C		E♭		G			
	1		♭3		5			

The following fingering pattern is perfect for the minor chord arpeggio because you can always start it with your first finger pointing at the root.

C Minor Arpeggio

G Minor Arpeggio

Example 4: Am-Dm-Bm-Em Arpeggios

This example demonstrates the minor arpeggio using the roots A, D, B and E. Like Example 3, Example 4 first gives the root only (Ex. 4A), then the minor arpeggio (Ex. 4B), next a slight variation of the arpeggio similar to a popular bass line (Ex. 4C) and finally a combination of these three techniques (Ex. 4D). This example also uses open string roots, so the fingering pattern is different than the "moveable fingering pattern." The diagram below shows the minor arpeggio with the open 3rd string (A) as the root.

A Minor Arpeggio

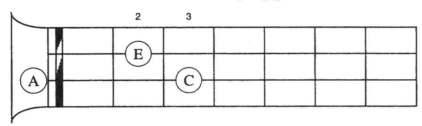

Example 4A — Root Only

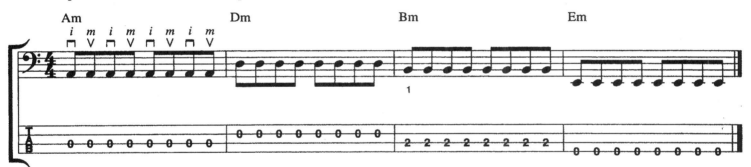

Example 4B — Minor Arpeggio

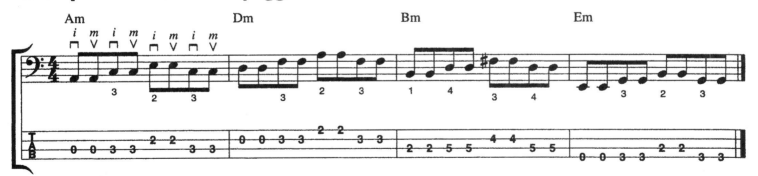

Example 4C — Rhythmic Variation

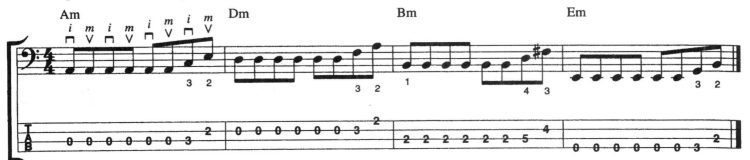

22

Example 4D — Compilation

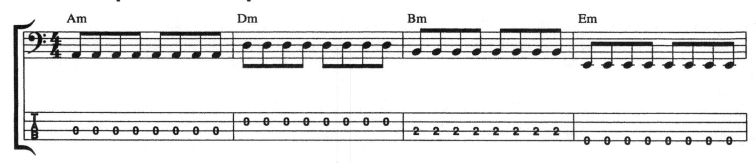

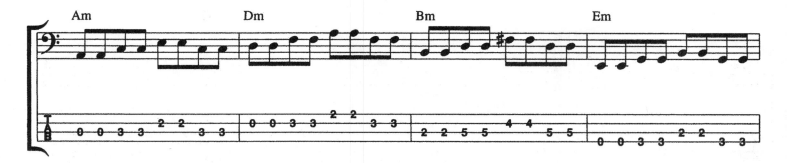

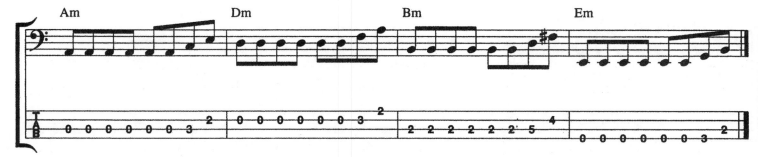

Practice repeating each individual chord separately to help develop technique and confidence.

Example 5

This example uses both major and minor chord arpeggios, and is based on a popular chord progression. A chord progression is a series of particular chords following a certain pattern. This particular progression can be found in songs such as "Blue Moon" and "Heart and Soul."

Example 5A

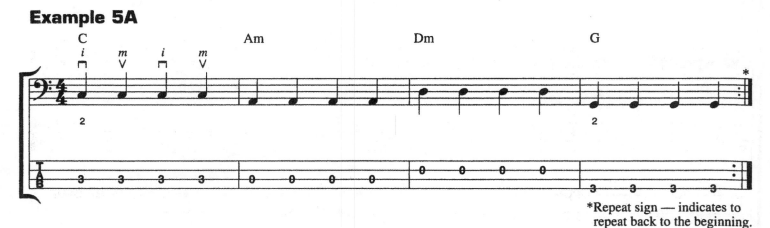

*Repeat sign — indicates to repeat back to the beginning.

Example 5B

Example 5C

Example 5D

For further study on arpeggios, practice identifying the major and minor arpeggios all over the neck. Just be sure to use the same patterns and be able to identify the root.

PLAYING WITH A DRUMMER

As members of a band, the bassist and drummer need to be a tight, indivisible team. The bass player needs to be sure that what he plays locks in with what the drummer is playing. One way to do this is to focus in on one particular part of the drum kit, such as the bass drum or snare, and play so that it and the bass sound as one instrument. Following are several common patterns to help you practice this.

Example 6: Ballad pattern

This first pattern is a common ballad feel. Play the root of the C chord with the bass drum (Ex. 6A), then when that feels comfortable, play the fifth of the C chord (G) with the snare (Ex. 6B), and finally, alternate between the two patterns (Ex. 6C).

Example 6A

Example 6B — Adding 5th (G) with Snare

Example 6C — Variation

The previous example is a very common bass line to use when playing ballads: the root to the fifth above. However, the fifth can also be played below the root. The lower fifth is played on the same fret as the root, on the next lowest string. For example, the fifth of the C chord can be found on the third fret of the E string.

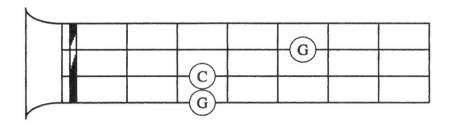

The fifths on the E string and D string are the same note, only an octave (8 notes) apart.

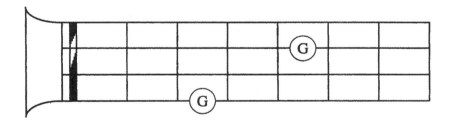

Example 7: Country Pattern

One style that uses the fifth below the root is Country. This exercise uses the root with the bass drum (Ex. 7A), then adds the fifth below, this time also with the bass drum (Ex. 7B), and finally combines the two previous examples (Ex. 7C).

Example 7A — Root with Bass Drum

*Indicates uneven eighth notes; listen to recorded example.

Example 7B — Adding 5th Below

Example 7C — Combination

Example 8: Latin Pattern

This pattern uses both the fifth above and below, and is commonly used in Latin bass lines. The first part of the example gives just the root (Ex. 8A), then adds the fifth above (Ex. 8B) and finally the fifth both above and below (Ex. 8C).

Example 8A — Root with Bass Drum/Latin

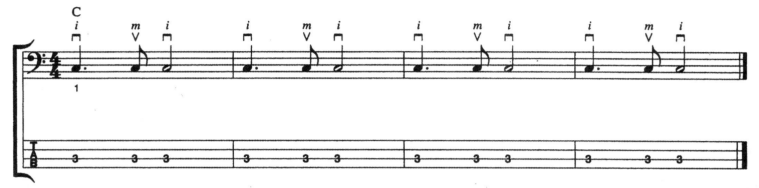

Example 8B — Adding 5th Above

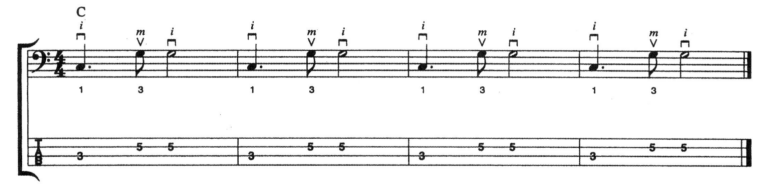

Example 8C — Adding 5th Above and Below

Work on alternating the picking hand and developing a clean attack. Practicing these exercises should help you to lock in with the drummer, but always use a metronome or drum machine to maintain consistent time.

Example 9

This exercise uses the root to the fifth, both above and below. The chord progression is common to many popular songs and can be played to many different rhythmic feels.

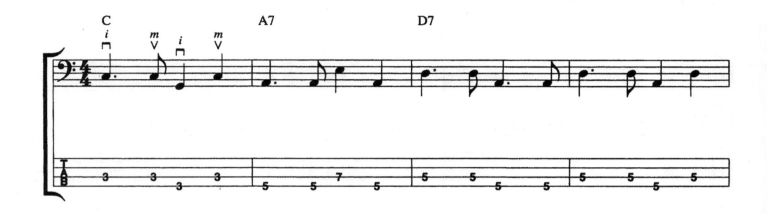

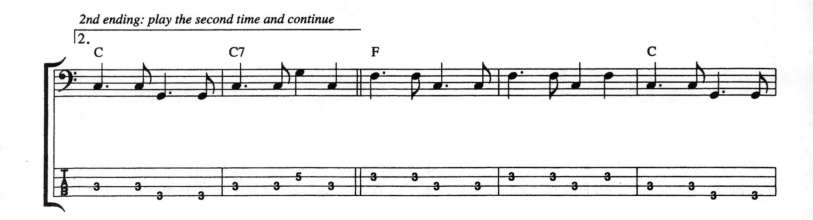

*The fermata indicates to hold the
note for an indefinite period of time.

Practice locating fifths above and below all notes on the neck, and familiarize yourself with
the patterns of both. Remember to keep alternating the right hand fingering.

PLAYIN' THE BLUES

The Blues is one of the most popular music styles. It's not very hard to play, but it is a lot of fun. It is a good idea to practice the blues, as most jam sessions usually contain at least one. A blues bass line is easy to get under your fingers initially, so you can start jamming right away.

Example 10

This example uses the G major chord arpeggio: root, third and fifth, but adds the sixth and flat seventh on the D string, walking up the notes and back down again. The sixth of a G major chord is six notes up the G major scale (G - A - B - C - D - E) and the flat seventh is seven notes up the G major scale (G - A - B - C - D - E - F#) lowered a half step to F♮. Note: When you "flat" the seventh, you lower it one half step. If F# is the seventh, then F is the flat seventh, not F♭.

G major scale:	G	A	B	C	D	E	F#	G
	1	2	3	4	5	6	7	8
G blues line:	G		B		D	E	F♮	
	1		3		5	6	♭7	

The first part of this example shows this bass line with G as the root (Ex. 10A), then with C as the root (Ex. 10B), with D as the root (Ex. 10C) and finally all three linked together in the typical blues progression (Ex. 10D).

Example 10A — G7 Blues Pattern

*Indicates Key of G major — all F's are sharp.

Example 10B — C7 Blues Pattern

Example 10C — D7 Blues Pattern

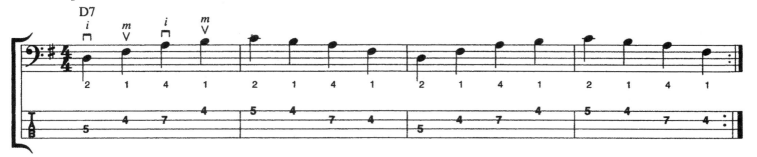

Example 10D — Combination Blues Patterns — Quarter Notes

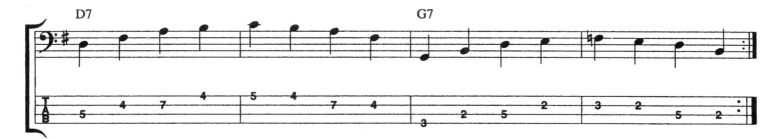

Example 11: *Combination Blues Pattern — Eighth Notes*

This example is similar to Example 10D, but uses eighth notes instead of quarter notes. Remember to alternate the right hand fingering.

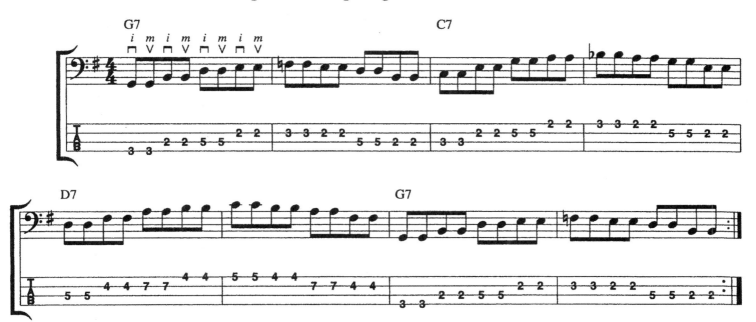

After mastering this bass line, try using it with different notes as the root. Simply start the pattern on a different note and keep the fingering and fret spacing the same.

Example 12: Complete Blues

This example uses what is called straight time, where the eighth notes are all even (the same length of time).

As you play, listen to the drummer and make sure that your even eighth notes are locked in with his eighth notes. Sometimes the drummer will play eighth notes on the hi-hat, sometimes on the ride cymbal, or fluctuations off the snare and the hi-hat, or the snare and the ride, but just focus on the groove and try to stay even and solid.

Example 13: Shuffle Blues

The next example uses the same pattern as Example 12, but uses shuffle time instead of straight time. In shuffle time, the eighth notes are no longer evenly spaced, as in straight time, but the first eighth note is a longer length of time than the second eighth note. This only affects the eighth notes, not the quarter notes. Listen to the recorded examples to help better distinguish between straight and shuffle eighth notes.

Example 14: 12-Bar Blues

A common blues progression is the 12-bar blues. This blues is 12 bars (measures) long and uses the G , C and D chords. Also, the last two bars contain the turnaround. The turnaround comes at the end of a song, and is a chord or series of chords which helps to indicate the end of the form by "turning it around" to the beginning. This turnaround uses a chromatic (all half steps) approach from the third of the G chord (B) to the root of the D chord (D).

After working on the 12-bar blues in G, try playing it around the neck in other keys, keeping the same relationship between the notes.

Example 15

Example 15 is a variation of the 12-bar blues and is typical of most rock and roll songs. This example incorporates a similar blues riff as used in the 12-bar blues, but varies the pattern a bit. It is also transposed to the key of A, so the open string notes are used.

*Indicates Key of A major — all F's, C's and G's are sharp.

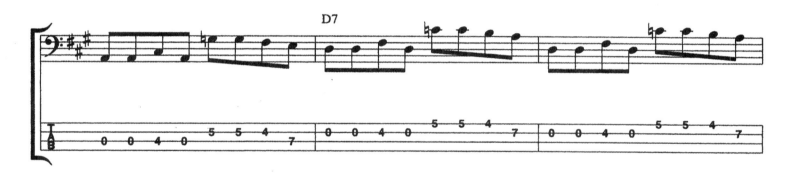

SLAP/POP TECHNIQUE

This technique of playing the bass has become very popular in recent years, and mainly consists of learning to think percussively (like a drummer). The first step is to be able to find the octaves on the bass, An octave is eight notes away from the root, and has the same note as the root. The octave from any note can be found by moving two strings up and two frets forward. Practice finding all the octaves on the E and A strings by starting with the open strings and working up the neck chromatically.

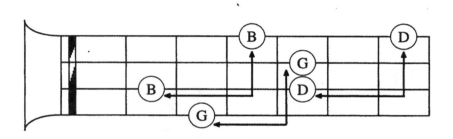

Example 16: The Slap

The next step in this technique is the slap, which is handled by the right hand thumb. The thumb acts like a hammer, striking the string with the outside of the knuckle, near the area on the bass where the neck meets the body. This can be varied for different sounds; for instance, by slapping further back towards the bridge over the pickups gives a brighter, much more open sound, while slapping directly over the neck gives a thinner, tighter sound. The thumb strikes the string, but does not lay on the string. It snaps back away from the string, allowing it to vibrate. Practice slapping the open strings to help establish a good thumb tone.

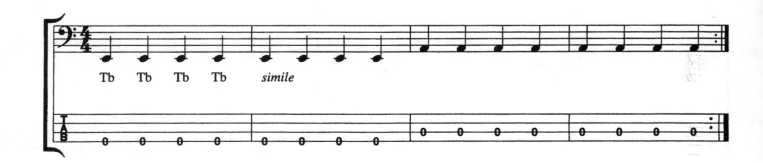

Example 17: The Pop

The final step to learning this technique is the pop, which is done with the right-hand index finger. This is achieved by pulling the string with the tip of the index finger, snapping it away from the fingerboard.

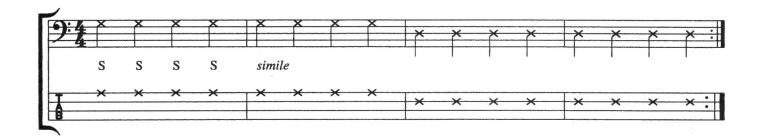

Example 18

This example combines the slap and the pop together. The first part alternates with one slap and one pop. Work on making the slap/pop technique one fluent motion, rather than two separate motions. As the thumb hammers down, the index finger moves into position to snap the string up, moving the hand back into its starting position.

Example 18A — Combining Slap and Pop

The next part of this example uses a variation of this technique, combining two slaps together. Since this technique has a very percussive feel to it, try to match what the drummer is playing by matching the slap with the drummer's bass drum and the pop with the drummer's snare. This example uses one slap and one pop, then two slaps and one pop.

Example 18B — Variation

Example 19

This example uses the previous technique, but is played over a chord progression, slapping the roots of the chords on the E and A strings and popping the octaves on the D and G strings. The exercise starts with the basic slap/pop technique (Ex. 19A), then incorporates the variation in the right hand (Ex. 19B) and finally a combination of the two (Ex. 19C).

Example 19A — Octave Exercise

Example 19B — Variation

Example 19C — Combination

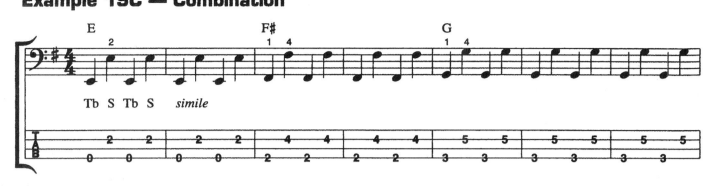

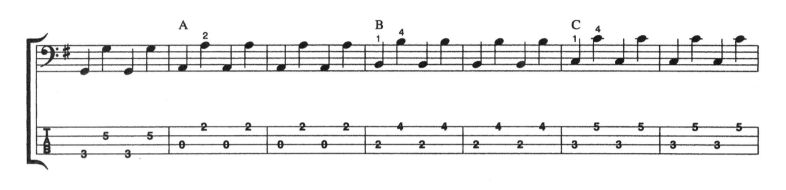

Example 20: The Hammer-on

This example uses a technique known as the hammer-on, where the note is sounded by hammering the string to the fretboard using the tip of any finger of the left hand. The note sounds by the left hand attack (the right hand is not used). Some strength in the left hand is required to perform this technique, practice it daily so the left and right hand attacks sound similar. It is also important to relax; hammering too hard will result in a poor sound.

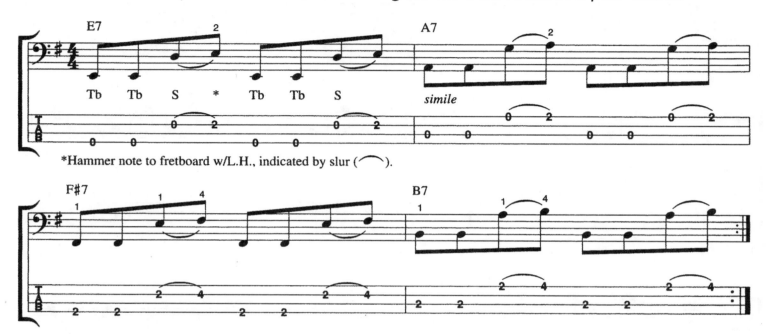

*Hammer note to fretboard w/L.H., indicated by slur (⌒).

Example 21: The Pull-off

The pull-off is also a left hand attack technique. Pull the string with the left hand finger tip as it lifts off the fingerboard (similar to plucking the string with the right hand). Again, practice until the pull-off sounds similar to the right hand attack.

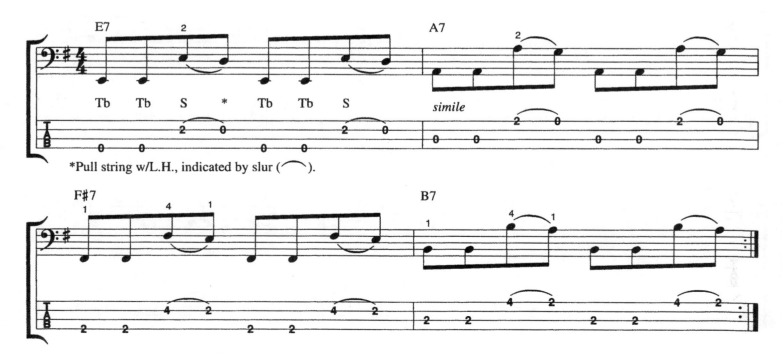

*Pull string w/L.H., indicated by slur (⌒).

Example 22

This example combines the hammer-on and pull-off techniques. If you're unable to keep with the video, practice at a slower tempo with a metronome or drum machine and build up the tempo gradually.

BLUES BASS

Basic Theory and Definitions

Here is a brief compendium of fundamental harmony and scale theory that is referred to as it applies to the bass guitar. Whether a new topic or simply a refresher for you, this material is beneficial in understanding most of the text and examples used. A more in depth study would elaborate on each of the examples but the following will provide an elementary introduction to basic theory.

Interval: Distance between two notes, whether played together or in succession

Interval of a minor third: three semi-tones (frets)

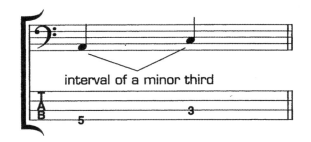

interval of a minor third

Interval of a major third: four semi-tones (frets)

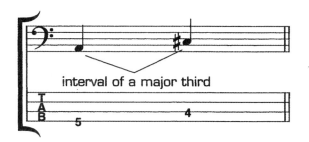

interval of a major third

Chord: A combination of three or more different notes

Triad: A combination of three notes consisting of any note with the interval of a major or minor 3rd and a 5th above

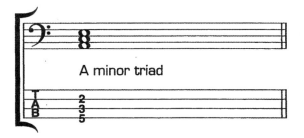

A minor triad

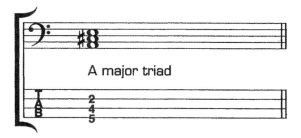

A major triad

Arpeggio: A chord which is played melodically; notes sounding consecutively

A minor arpeggio

A major arpeggio

Four part chord: A triad with a major 7th or ♭7th degree added

Scale: A series of notes rising and/or falling, according to some system, usually encompassing an octave

Pentatonic scale: A five note scale

Major pentatonic scale: A five note scale containing root, second, third, fifth and sixth

Minor pentatonic scale: Contains the same notes as the major pentatonic scale but starts on the 6th degree

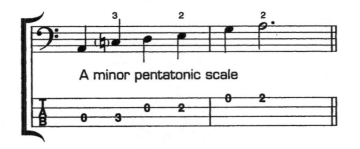

Blues scale: A minor pentatonic scale with a flatted 5th between the 4th and 5th degrees

Equipment

Blues songs usually require a solid, full bass sound. Bass and guitar players can choose between a passive or an active instrument. An active instrument means that its pickups are powered by a battery whereas a passive does not require any. It is a matter of taste which type of bass you play as well as how you amplify your instrument. You can use a tube amplifier, pre-amp or a solid state amplifier to broadcast your groove but you will hear which type of equipment best meets or suits the authenticity of the blues.

You have a choice of round wound or unwound strings as well. Wound strings encompass a steel string core that is fully covered with a thin, tightly wrapped strand of nickel or equivalent metal. Unwound strings are not covered. String gauges vary but a typical set could comprise of a .045mm for a first (G string) to .105mm for a 4th string. After experimentation you will more than likely adhere to whatever plays and sounds the best for you. You may even include a "5 string" bass as part of your set up. The 5th string, a low "B," gives you an extended harmonic range and is very flexible and efficient for your position playing.

Photo courtesy of Schecter Guitar Research

Photo courtesy of Schecter Guitar Research

The 12-Bar Blues Progression

It is essential that you familiarize yourself with the 12-bar blues form. The earliest rural blues relies on the basic I-IV-V chord progression. The chords are derived from the three primary triads of the major scale. However, the addition of the ♭7th degree to each chord adds to the tension and dominant quality of the progression. The basic blues form consists of four bars of the I chord, two bars of the IV chord, two bars of the I chord again, two bars of the V chord and finally two bars of the I chord (see below). This 12-bar succession of chords usually repeats itself over and over again, enlisting the improvisational skills of the musicians.

A variation of this progression has been called the "quick change" blues progression. For more harmonic interest, the IV chord is introduced briefly in measure 2. Then return to the I chord. In the tenth bar, the IV chord is reinstated after the V chord before returning to the I chord in measure 11. In the final bar, measure 12, a "turnaround" is created by playing the V chord, which acts as a springboard and simply sets up the entire progression for repetition.

12-Bar Blues

*These chords are used in the "quick change" blues progression.

Shuffle Blues Bass Lines

Most of the examples in this book are played in the "shuffle" or 12/8 feel. A shuffle feel is created from the triplet figure, (♪♪♪) three eighth notes played in the time it takes to play two eighth notes or a quarter note. The first two notes, however, are tied together (♪♪♪). Songs written with a shuffle feel will have a shuffle indication at the beginning. This means that although the eighth notes are written normally (♪♪) they are played in the triplet feel (♪♪).

Example 23: Roots and Triads

The first example is a shuffle that Elmore James popularized but Robert Johnson may have invented. The bass line reinforces the chord progression with simple quarter note roots on the I, IV and V chords for the first "chorus." (A chorus in the blues genre is one complete 12-bar cycle of the chord progression.)

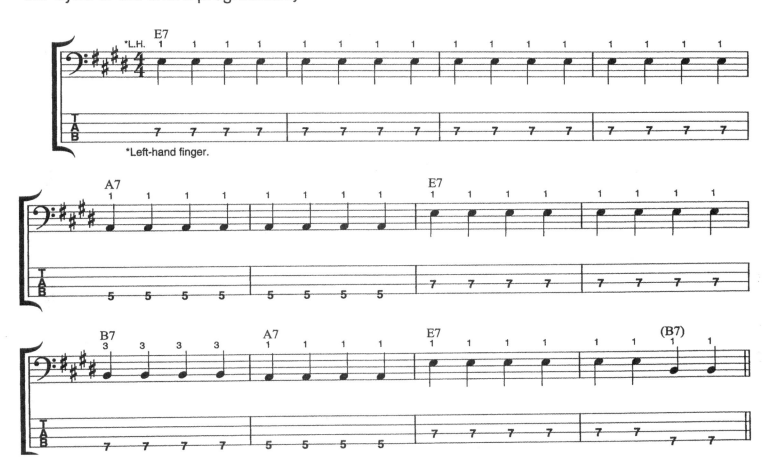

The second chorus in this example is based on simple "triads" of each chord. (A major triad consists of the root, the major 3rd and the 5th of a chord.) For example, the foundation of the I chord "E" is: E (the root), G# (the major 3rd) and B (the 5th).

Chorus 2:

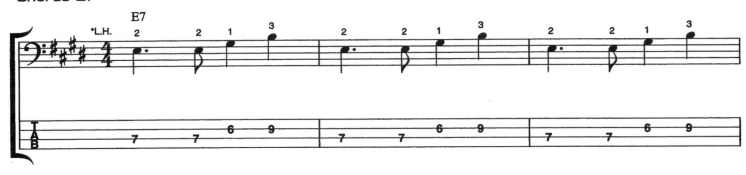

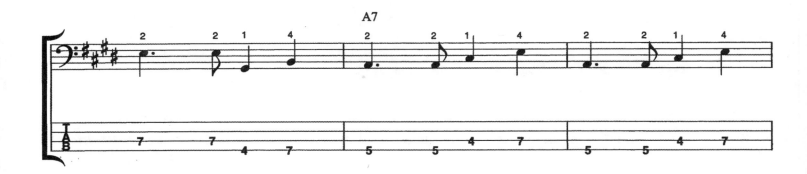

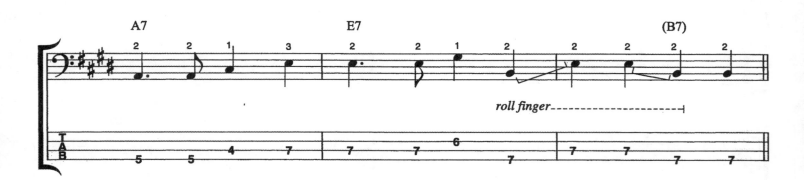

The third chorus is supported by "root/5th" activity in the bass using eighth notes. It returns to familiar territory with simple quarter note roots for the final chorus. Watch your left hand fingering when you play the third chorus; when playing two notes with the same finger, roll that finger from string to string, play both notes staccato (detached). Don't let them "ring" into each other.

Chorus 3:

Chorus 4:

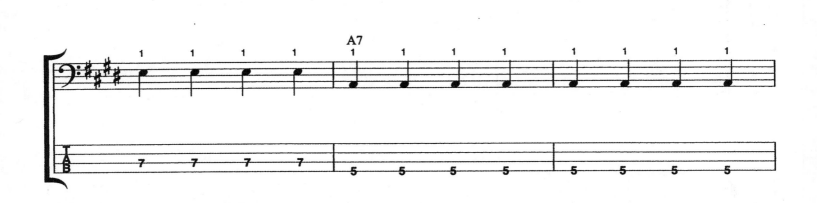

Example 24: The 6th Degree

This example is an extension of the triad idea; it introduces a fourth tone, the major sixth of the chord. For the G chord the sixth is "E," for the C chord the sixth is "A" and for the D chord the sixth is "B."

52

Example 25: Muted Notes

Practice Example 25 and then play Example 26 with the band. Try this example as an alternative to Example 24. Instead of playing the second eighth note (the pickup to the downbeat) as a real note, fake or "mute" it. Do this by not actually fretting the note, instead lightly touching the string with your left hand. You can achieve this effect anywhere on the neck. Use it as an accent or "pickup" to propel the music along. In addition to adding to the feel of a tune, it facilitates your position shifts because you are not committed to playing the "actual" note before you make your hand shift.

*Muted note.

Example 26

Example 27: Dropped Octave

Yet another variation of the triad with the added sixth tone is suggested in this line in the key of C. By dropping down an octave to the 5th of the chord (G) in the second and fourth measures, it reinforces the tonic (C) on the first beat. Listen to Example 27A and play with the band.

Example *27A*

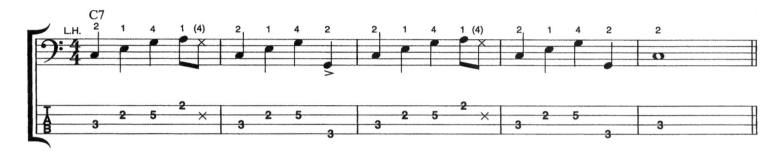

Example *27B*

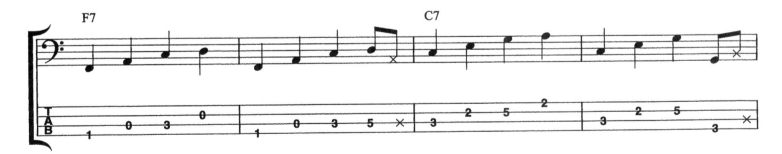

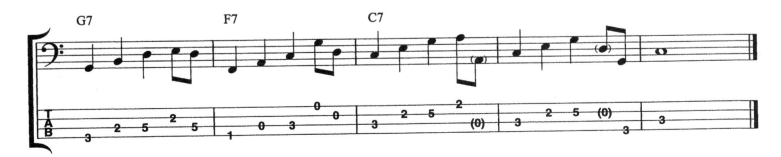

Example 28: Chromatic Passing Tone

Here we have the introduction of non-chord and non-scale notes. The G♭ (F♯) is referred to as a "chromatic" passing tone and lies between the root (G) and the ♭7th (F) of the G7 chord. A chromatic note (C♯) bridges the 4th (C) and the 5th (D) as well. Note that each of these "passing tones" is an eighth note and does not appear on a strong beat ("1," "2," "3" or "4").

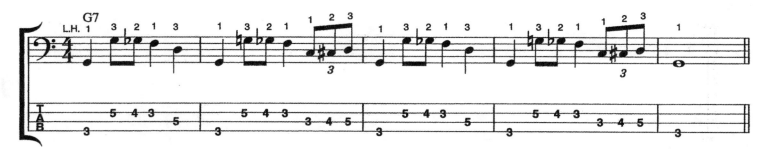

Example 29: Triplets

Once you have the previous study under your fingertips, play along with the band in this example.

Example 30

Example 30 is simply a variation using triplets on every fourth beat

56

Example 31: Memphis/Jimmy Reed Feel

This familiar line is referred to as the "Memphis" or "Jimmy Reed" feel. It is distinguishable by what the guitarist plays. Namely, in this example in the key of A, he plays A5, A6, A7 and back to A6 — two beats per chord. This bass line outlines an A7 chord over two bars with an accented octave, A, on the third beat. Transpose this hip idea to as many "blues" keys as you can.

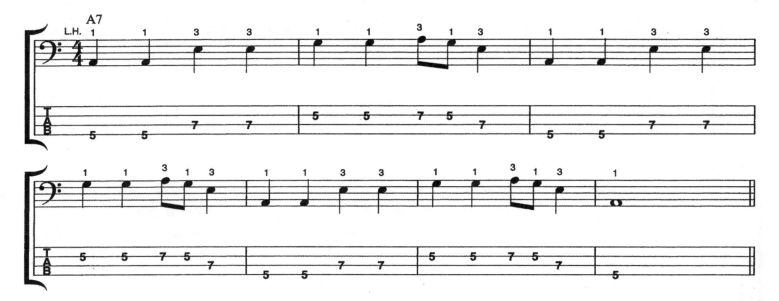

Example 32: Open String Bass

Examples 32A and 32B are the same bass line, first in G and then in the key of E with open strings. Pay particular attention to muting the open strings so they don't ring on through the phrase.

Example 32A

Example 32B

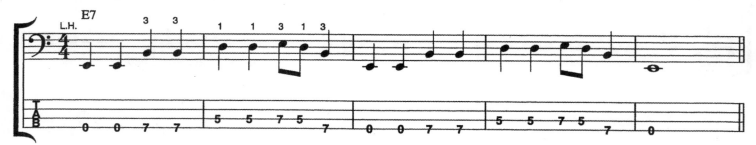

Example 33: 2/2 or Cut Time

Example 33 is your chance to use some of the bass lines covered so far with the band. The two choruses have been written in 2/2 or "cut time." This means that there are two strong beats to a measure. You could count quickly in common time (4/4) and simply refer to the snare drum as it strikes beats two and four while you tap your foot on beats one and three. This is why the form of the progression looks twice as long as we have been used to. It is somewhat of a precursor to the next topic.

58

Two Beat Blues Feel

The "two beat blues feel" actually evokes a half time feel over common time measures. It can be heard as a "New Orleans style march feel". In the first measure of Example 34, half notes outline the chord with a simple root/five. But the second bar uses the sixth degree on the 4th beat to end the little "two bar" phrase.

Example 34: New Orleans Style March Feel

Example 35

Here we use our "muted note" technique to enhance this little gem. On the "and" of beat three in the second bar, release the fretted note (C) just enough to get a muted sound before striking beat four.

This can be a very effective way of pushing the groove along. You should get the idea once you play through Example 36 .

Example 36

The Slow Blues

Probably the most familiar sound in all the blues is the "slow blues." The 12-bar patterns in this section are based on the dominant 7th (♭7th) chord. In the key of G, G is the root, B is the major 3rd, D is the 5th and F is the ♭7th. In the following examples, a few non-chord tones, which we referred to as "chromatics", are used as passing tones.

Example 37: Using The ♭7th

In Example 37, a G7 chord is outlined with a passing tone on the 4th beat inside a triplet. The triplet is the essence of the pulse of the "slow blues" and by playing it on the 4th beat emphasizes the groove.

Example 38: Using A Simple Triad

In Example 38A, a simple but effective triad lays claim to the bassline. But in Example 16B, a powerful triplet on the second beat covers the 3rd and 5th of G as it leads to the ♭7th, F.

Example 38A

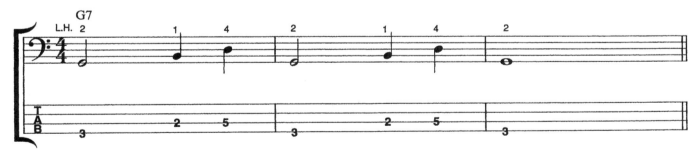

Example 38B: Triplets (12/8 feel)

Example 39: Walking The Bass

This next example involves a technique along the lines of how a jazz bass player would approach a standard blues. "Walking the bass" involves a combination of chord-scale and passing-tones played in quarter notes. Chromatic tones are usually resolved by a half step, meaning that they are only a semi-tone away from a strong scale or chord tone.

Example 40

Listen carefully to the band in this example then play along. A very strong triplet feel dominates each of the five choruses. The last one is a composite of the preceding techniques. Notice the brief interaction in bar four (G7) by the drummer and bass.

63

64

Minor Blues

The minor blues is another very popular sound of the blues, especially with the slow 12/8 feel. The chords are still I-IV-V but are now minor instead of major. This simply means that all the I, IV and V chords are minor rather than major or dominant.

The minor blues can be played several different ways, often resembling a slow blues in a major key. The only difference is that the bass line in a minor blues often employs a minor 7th **arpeggio** (the notes of the related chord played one at a time in succession).

Example 41: Minor 7th Arpeggios

Example 41A is a bass line over A minor7 with a 12/8 feel and is a prelude to Example 41B. Notice that the bass simply arpeggiates the chord changes to each bar.

Example 41A

Example 41B

Example 42: "Green Onions" Style

This next example is a bass line with the same chords; Am7-Dm7-Em7. You may recognize it as the bass line from a tune called "Green Onions" by Booker T. and the M.G.'s as well as "Help Me" by Sonny Boy Williamson. This time the fourth degree is used momentarily as an eighth note on the first half of the fourth beat. In the previous examples where the bass line does not include the major or minor third degree but relies mainly on movement between the ♭7th, 5th and/or 4th degree, the line can work equally as well over a minor blues progression.

Example 43

Listen to Example 43. It is the same bass line as Example 30, the only difference between the two is in the chord harmony. The following is in a minor key.

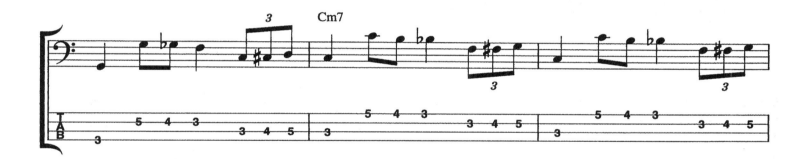

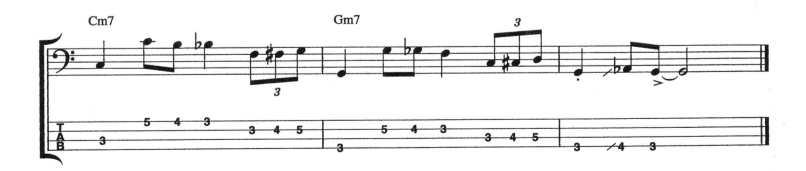

Example 44: Fever Style

By staying in the 12/8 shuffle mode and in the key of A minor we play a two measure minor 7th line reminiscent of a tune called "Fever."

Example 45

Play along with Example 45. It is a simple but very effective line.

Example 46: The Thrill Is Gone

One of the most popular and enduring blues progressions of the last twenty-five years is "The Thrill Is Gone" by B.B. King. It is a 12-bar minor blues and a little different than any example so far. The difference arrives at the ninth and tenth measures. Instead of going to the minor V chord in bar nine, the resolution is delayed by the insertion of the major VI chord (G) followed by a dominant V7 chord (F♯7), which resolves back to the Im7 (Bm7). The bass line from this B.B. King classic outlines the root, 4th, 5th and ♭7th of each chord. Basic, but again extremely effective!

Alternative Styles

Like jazz music, the blues has absorbed other musical influences. For example, styles such as "rhythm and blues" evolved from early rural blues and in turn have influenced today's blues music. Latin music has even left it's signature on the blues. The following bass-line examples typify a few of those blues "grooves" that you may come across.

Example 47: The Latin Surf

Example 47 can be described as a "Latin/surf" beat. The line spells out the root and the ♭7th of the chord, with the assistance of a chromatic push by the major 7th to the root. Because no major or minor third is present, the line can be played over a major or minor progression.

Example 48

A similar line is shown in Example 48. Note that it contains ideas we have already learned from previous examples; the "muted" note on the second beat and the "chromatic passing tone" on the fourth beat. The line centers around the root, 5th and the ♭7th. This is inspired from a tune called "Born In Chicago" from the first Paul Butterfield Blues Band album.

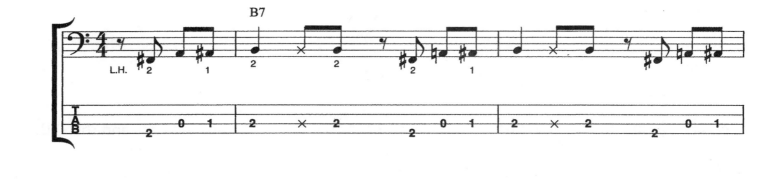

Example 49

Play along with this example to "feel the groove." Watch the last two measures in particular. The very last bar is played with a "band cue." This means that the ending or last note is played via a mutually agreed upon signal. It is usually accomplished with a simple nod or similar gesture.

73

Example 50: The Latin/Rhumba Feel

This next example is a Latin/rhumba type feel using the root, major 3rd, 5th and 6th degree from the chord. This bass line is influenced by a tune called "Cross Cut Saw" by Albert King. The "syncopated" beats (the "and" of "2" and "3") draw out the Latin/rhumba feel. Again the bass guitar follows the standard blues progression in the key of A♭ major.

Example 51

Play Example 51 and memorize this line in different keys.

49

Example 52: Bo Diddly Style

Here is a bass line that is not very challenging harmonically but makes up for that deficiency in its rhythm. It is in the realm of guitarist "Bo Diddly" and adheres to the basic root, its octave and occasionally the ♭7th. It has a quasi-Latin ambiance to it and is propelled again with the "muted" note. This note is played on an open third string to create movement. Practice Example 52A a few times before playing Example 52B with the band. The example has been written here in 2/2 (cut time) to facilitate reading with simple quarter and eighth notes. The form looks twice as long as the usual 12-bar progression.

Example 53: '60s R&B/Soul

This example shows us the kind of effect '60s Rhythm and Blues and soul music has had on the blues. Stalwart bass players like James Jamerson and Chuck Rainey had an enormous impact on the music at that time and it is revealed in these syncopated lines. The two measure line falls nicely over each chord change except when we get to the ninth and tenth bars; here we have a different chord for each measure. So a little quick thinking will reveal that if you play the first half of the two-bar line on the V chord (E7) at bar nine, and then the second half of the line which you played over the IV (D) chord over measure ten, you will resolve nicely to the I (A7) chord at bar eleven. Whew! It is much easier to play than to read. So, run through this example a few times before playing with the band at Example 54.

Example 54

Play Along

Example 55: "A7 Funk Jam"

This is an open jam for you to explore the bass lines from Example 54. There are six choruses here with the ending written out. The actual bass guitar track you hear is intentionally ambiguous as it imitates a second electric guitar part and tries to stay clear of your playing.

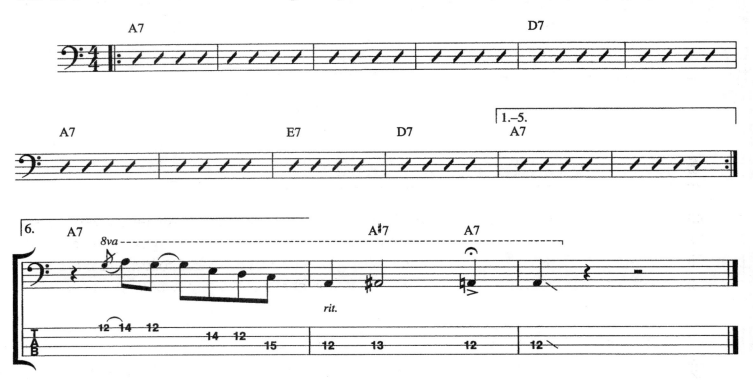

Example 56: "Shuffle Jam"

This is a "shuffle" for you to try some more of the ideas presented in this book. Again the actual bass guitar on the track echoes a second electric guitar. There are seven choruses for you to ad lib. and create a solid bass line. Note the G minor "pentatonic scale" played by the bass guitar on the ending.

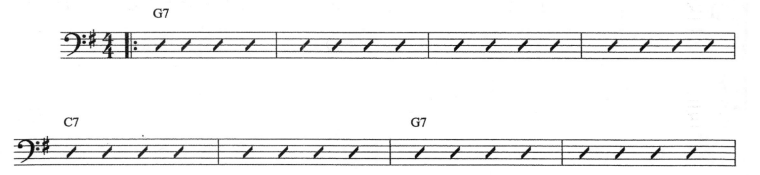

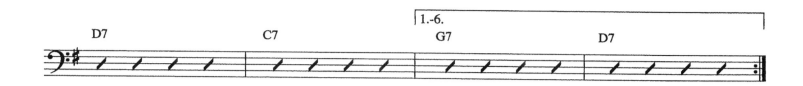

Example 57: "Big Boss Man"

This number is played with additional support by keyboard and vocals. It is similar to "Big Boss Man," and it is a prime example of the "Memphis/Jimmy Reed feel" similar to Example 31. This one is in the key of E major and written in "cut time." You should be able to follow the bass player as he sticks close to a familiar line. There are four choruses with the ending included.

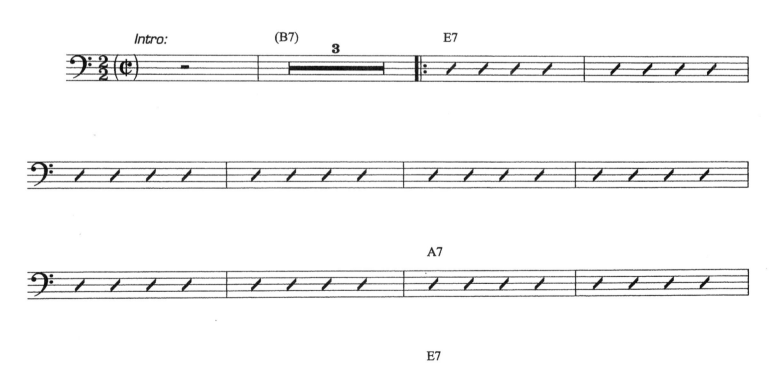

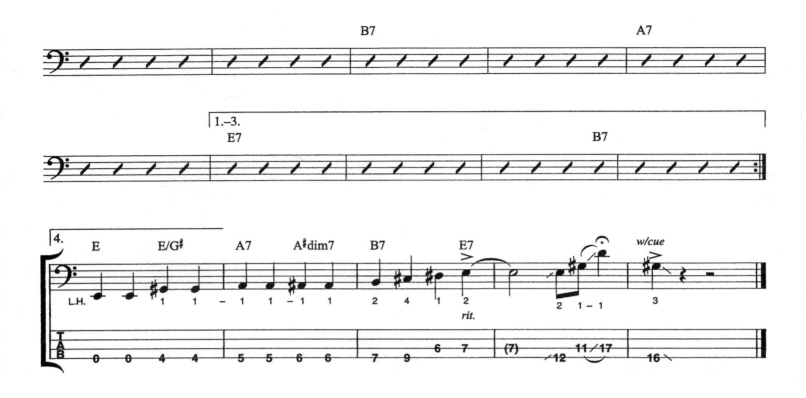

Example 58: "Help Me"

Here is an A minor blues similar to "Help Me" by Sonny Boy Williamson. It exemplifies the natural minor blues we covered earlier. Actually it is the same progression as Example 42. There are seven choruses for you to play along before it fades out.

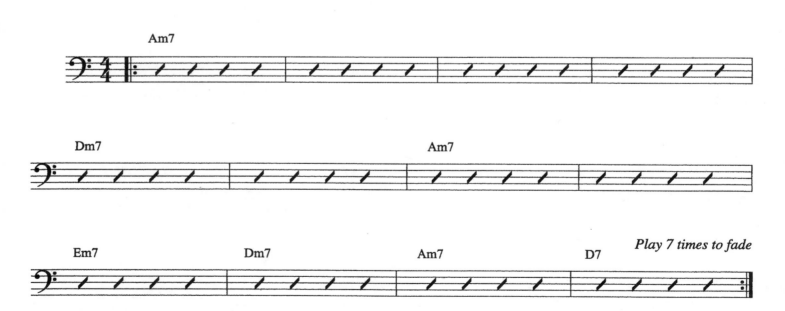

Example 59: "Everyday I Have The Blues"

This jazz/blues example is similar to "Everyday I Have The Blues." We haven't explored this particular chord sequence in detail but the chord chart is easy to follow. The bass outlines the chords with the "walking bass" technique we studied previously. The chords in this chart are written with basic ♭7th chords even though the piano and guitar actually play extensions of the basic harmony. Listen extensively to the bass player as he uses solid quarter notes to walk through the nine choruses. The ending has been written out.

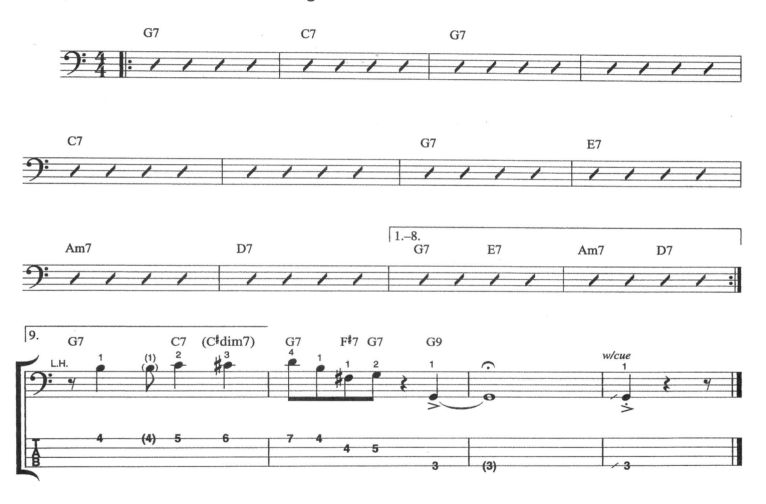

The key to really mastering the blues is to "get out there and play." Listen to recordings by the original blues artists that created the styles that we have covered as well as the blues players from the '40s, '50s and '60s. There is a wealth of information to be learned.

Play and "jam" with friends and/or put a band together. Try to find every opportunity you can to play your bass.

ROCK BASS

Rock Bass
Introduction

This section will show you some classic rock grooves and bass lines that every rock bass player needs to know, various right- and left-hand techniques, quarter, eighth, and sixteenth note feels, how to work rhythmically with a drummer, and some special techniques, such as harmonics, tapping and double-stops. All of the classic bass lines are also included on the video for you to hear and play along with.

RIGHT HAND TECHNIQUES

When playing the examples, there are several different tone qualities that you can create with your right hand without ever touching the tone control knob on your bass or amplifier. This is done by positioning the right hand at various places on the bass and is necessary to achieve the correct sound for the style you are playing.

When playing ballads and long notes, such as whole and half notes, play up near the neck; this gives a full, rich sound.

When playing quarter and eighth note feels, play directly over the pickups; this gives a more percussive sound.

When playing sixteenth note feels, play back by the bridge; this gives a thinner, tighter sound with more definition.

ROCK BALLAD FEELS

Throughout this section we will cover many different classic rock grooves; some of them are fast sixteenth note rock feels, others are slow ballads and some even use power chords. Each one will help develop the techniques that you will need to know as a rock bass player. One of the most important things you need to be able to do as a rock bass player is to lock in with the drummer. This is done by matching the subdivision (the way each beat is subdivided) the drummer is projecting. Play along with the video to practice locking in.

Example 60: Slow Ballad

This example demonstrates a slow ballad feel in the key of G major. A ballad is usually characterized as having a slow tempo and sad or melancholy quality. The example alternates between the root of the I chord (G) and the vi chord (Em), using a dotted quarter to eighth note feel. There is also a connecting line leading from the root of each chord, moving down chromatically from the G to the E and back up chromatically from the E to the G. This gives the line a little character in addition to connecting the roots of the chords. A chromatic connecting line moves up or down by half steps, sounding every pitch between the roots. Use your left hand to achieve separation between the notes by releasing the pressure on the string, lifting the string off of the fretboard to stop it from ringing.

Example 61: "Stand By Me" Ballad

This example is another ballad feel. This one is similar to the song "Stand By Me" by Ben E. King. It is in the key of C major and moves in a standard I (C), vi (Am), IV (F), V (G) chord progression. To help make a smooth transition between the roots of the chords, this example uses **diatonic** rather than chromatic connecting lines (meaning the notes are from a particular scale, in this case C major).

Scales

Before moving on to the next example, there are two scales that you are going to need to know. As a rock bassist, you are going to find you do not need to know that many scales, but these two are very important. They are the major and minor pentatonic scales, and they contain the five primary notes from the major and minor scales.

First is the **major pentatonic**, which uses the root, second, third, fifth and sixth of the major scale.

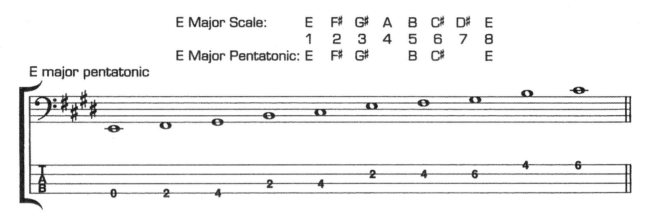

Next is the **minor pentatonic**, which uses the root, third, fourth, fifth and seventh of the minor scale.

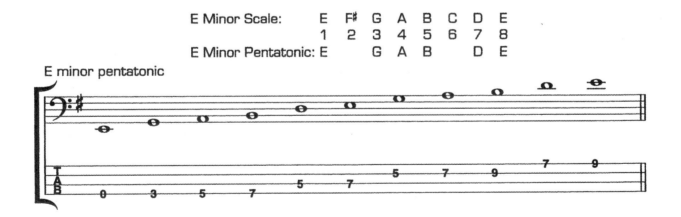

Both scales are demonstrated here using E as the root, but can be transposed to use any note as the root.

Example 62: "My Girl" Riff

This example uses the E and A major pentatonic scales, starting on the root and ascending to the octave. It is based on the immortal bass line of the popular tune "My Girl" by the Temptations. It also contains a common line that walks down from the V chord (B7) to the I (E) which brings you back to the top of the song. This is sometimes called the **turnaround**.

This example transposes the "My Girl" riff to E minor, giving it a darker, heavier sound.

Minor pentatonic "My Girl" riff:

Example 63: Ballad with Passing Tones

This is another example of a ballad that uses passing tones. It starts on the I chord (E), walks down the major scale to the vi chord (C#m) with the D# as a passing tone, then down to the IV chord (A) with the B as a passing tone, then down to the ii chord (F#m) with the G# as a passing tone, then walks up the E major scale, using the A# and D♮ as chromatic passing tones. This chord progression is very common and can be found in many popular rock and country ballads.

Example 64

This example is a ballad feel in the key of C, introducing what is known as the **slash chord** (G/B). A slash chord occurs when the bass note is not the root of the chord, but is instead another chord tone, such as the third or fifth. This example uses several slash chords such as the G/B chord, where the bass is playing B (the third of the G chord), not the root. The example primarily descends through the C major scale and uses mostly half notes. Be sure to make the "right hand feel" consistent and all the notes the same length. Listen to, and lock in with, the drummer.

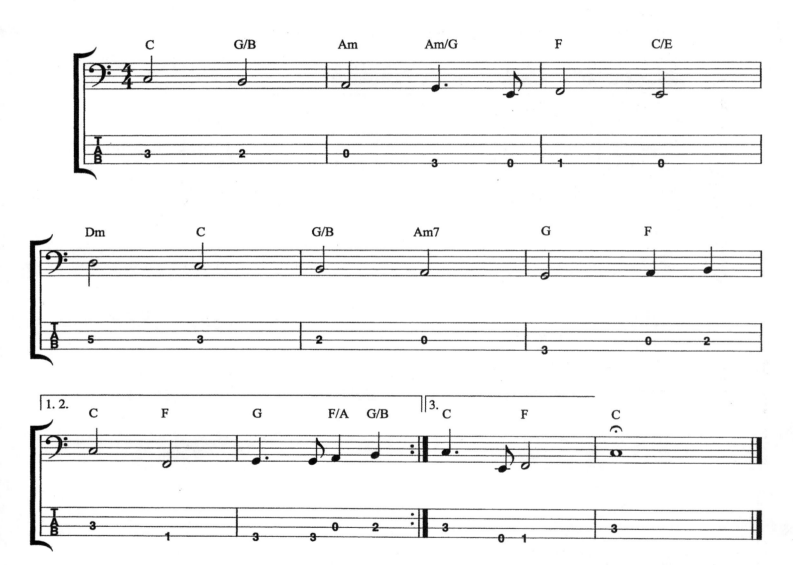

QUARTER NOTE ROCK FEELS

This next section covers several quarter note rock feels. The feel of quarter note roots and simple lines is common to what is known as "stadium rock." When playing large venues, the bass player, when he or she gets too busy, will not be heard in the hall. Most of the exercises in this section concentrate on this quarter note feel.

Example 65

This example uses quarter note roots throughout, alternating between A and G. To keep the example interesting there are several eighth note lines connecting each chord change, leading up chromatically or down diatonically to the root of the next chord.

92

Example 66: Slide and Hammer-on

This next example uses two new techniques: the **slide** and the **hammer-on**. To slide from one pitch to another, simply play a note and slide your finger to the next note, keeping pressure on the string. The hammer-on is done by hammering the string to the fretboard using the tip of any left hand finger. The note is sounded by the left hand attack (the right hand is not used).

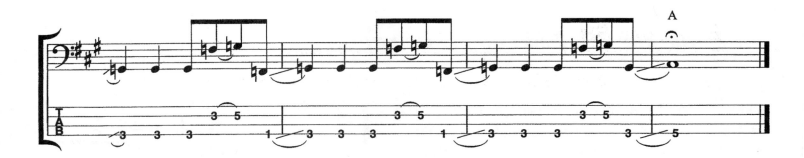

Example 67: "Rolling Stones Feel"

This example is very similar to many of the lines used by Rolling Stones bassist Bill Wyman. It uses the root, fifth and sixth of the chord, moving down then up the pattern. The pattern is based on the major pentatonic scale, using three of the five notes of the scale.

Example 68

This is very similar to Example 67, except it is based on the mirror, rather than the major, pentatonic scale. The pattern is played over a 12-bar minor blues—a common song form.

Example 69: Ostinato Bass

This example introduces a technique known as **ostinato bass**. Ostinato is a big word which basically means that while the chords move, the bass note doesn't. In this case the bass pedals an E underneath the chords, starting on the low E and then adding the octave above as the dynamic level of the song rises, to make the feel more intense. Remember to be consistent with the "right hand feel" so that each note sounds similar to the next.

Example 70

Here we use the major pentatonic scale in what is known as an "and" feel. This is also referred to as syncopation, where the notes are played primarily on the up-beats. The up-beats are in-between the beats, and are called "and" (1 and 2 and 3 and 4 and). This example plays on beat 1, and then on the "ands" of beats 2, 3 and 4.

Practice counting the rhythm aloud and listen to the recorded example to get the feel of the rhythm.

98

EIGHTH NOTE ROCK FEELS

This next section covers several eighth-note rock grooves. The exercises are similar to the exercises in the previous section in that they are mostly roots and simple passing lines, but using primarily eighth notes instead of quarter notes (two notes per beat instead of one). Be sure to alternate your left hand fingers when you practice to help increase your speed.

Example 71: "ZZ Top Groove"

This example uses a groove similar to a song by the legendary rock band ZZ Top. This one is mostly roots with a chromatic line approaching each chord change, giving the impression of a "walking" movement. The example also adds the II chord (Am) and ends with some upper register **double-stops** and **chords**. Double-stops refer to playing more than one note at a time and are usually done in the upper register of the bass due to the overall low range of the instrument. When lower range notes are played together, they tend to sound muddy and the pitches are hard to perceive.

Example 72

This example is the same as Example 71, except it is indicated to play the notes **staccato** (by the dots over and under the note heads). Staccato means that the note is cut off sharply by stopping the string from vibrating. This can be done by releasing the pressure in the left hand, lifting the finger slightly off of the fretboard but not off of the string. Playing staccato makes the feel much sharper.

Example 73

Here is an eighth note pattern in the key of E, using the root, fifth and flat seventh of the scale. To help solidify the groove there is a sixteenth note lick at the end of each phrase emulating a pattern played by the drums. The notes in this lick are muted. It is easier to play if the index finger is dragged across the strings, a technique commonly known as "raking."

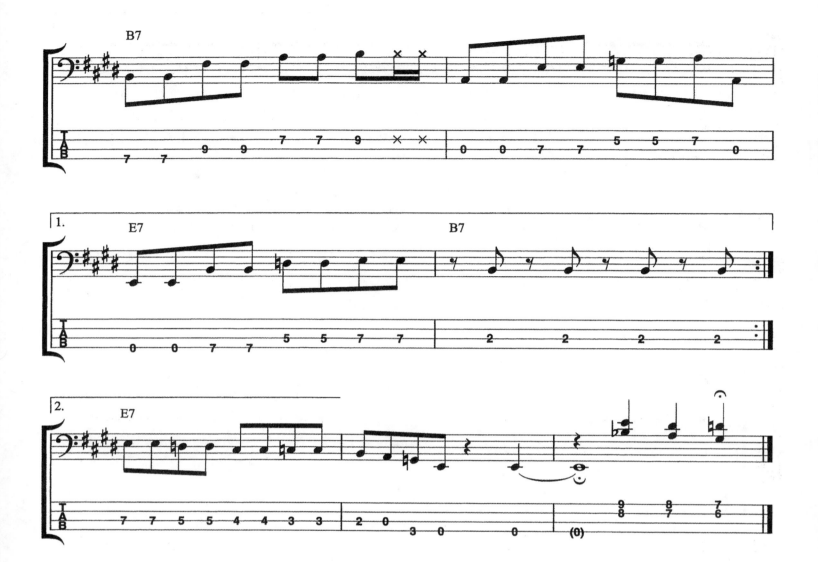

Example 74

This next eighth-note example can be divided into two sections. The first section uses ostinato bass (where the chords move but the bass note doesn't). In the second section, the bass line follows the chord changes, which makes the tune sound different. Remember to practice alternating the right hand fingers, keeping the notes steady and hitting the strings with the same finger pressure; that way the volume will be consistent.

103

Example 75

This one uses most of the notes in the major pentatonic scale plus the flat third. The technique of using both the minor and major third is very common to rock and blues. The example uses both **open** and **closed position**. Open position means the open strings are used and closed position means they are not used. To play both thirds in closed position, slide the left hand first finger up from the minor third to the major third (D - D♯).

SIXTEENTH NOTE ROCK FEELS

This section covers several sixteenth note feels. Sixteenth notes receive a quarter of a beat in 4/4 time. To count sixteenth notes, use the syllables "e" and "a" for the notes between the beats and up beats (1 e & a 2 e & a 3 e & a 4 e & a). A good example of a sixteenth note feel is the bass line from the song "Goin' Down" by Jeff Beck, shown in Example 76.

Example 76

In addition to the sixteenth-note feel, this example also uses a technique known as the **bend.** To bend the string, pull the fourth string down towards the third string until the pitch raises from A to B♭, then release the string to allow the pitch to return to A. It is helpful to use more than one finger in the left hand when bending a string, fretting the note with the third finger but keeping the first and second fingers on the string for support. Be sure to listen to make sure the bend is in tune.

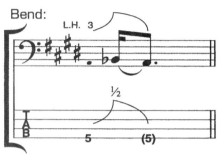

Example 77

This example is similar to many of the bass lines played by Rocco Prestia from Tower of Power. The sixteenth notes move up chromatically to the root (E) and fifth (B) via connecting lines. Practice the example slowly at first to develop a clean attack, then slowly speed up. Use a metronome or drum machine.

108

ROCK SHUFFLE AND BOOGIE FEELS

This next section deals primarily with rock shuffle feels. A shuffle is usually described as playing the eighth notes of a song with a triplet feel, where the eighth notes are played on the first and last part of the triplet. A triplet is playing three notes per beat and by cutting out the middle note, this gives you the shuffle feel. Shuffles are also written in 12/8 time, where there are 12 eighth notes per bar, grouped into four sets of three eighth notes. This is similar to playing four beats of triplets. Be sure to listen to the audio examples to hear the difference between the shuffle feels in this section and the "straight" feels in the previous sections.

Example 78

Here is a simple shuffle feel, using mostly roots and simple chromatic lines approaching the chord changes. Remember to alternate the right hand fingers. This will help to play the shuffle feel at faster tempos.

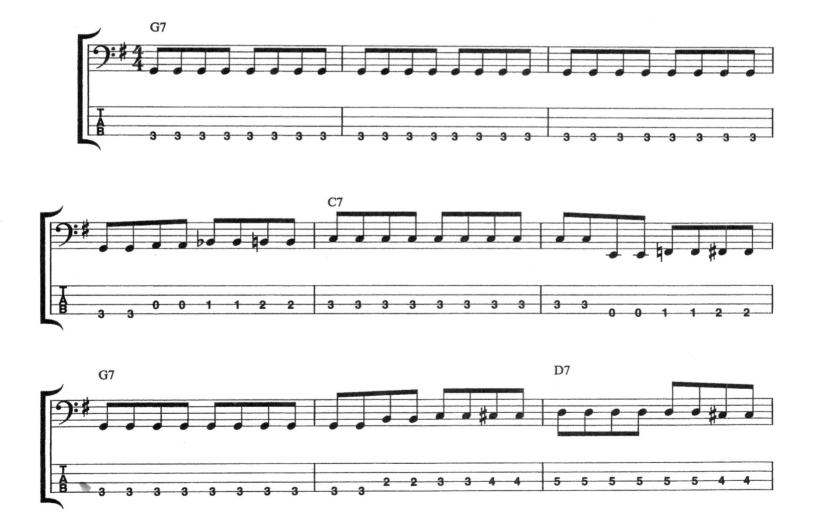

110

Example 79: Staccato Shuffle

Here is another shuffle that uses a staccato feel. Remember that to play staccato, simply lift the left hand finger off of the string for just a moment. You can see how the notes are cut off, which leaves just a tiny amount of space. That little bit of room between the notes makes the feel bounce just a little more than the legato feel.

Example 80

This example introduces another hammer-on technique, where the notes are sounded by hammering the string to the fretboard rather than the right hand attack. This example uses a triplet hammer-on in the left hand. The note is sounded by the right hand attack, then the second finger hammers on, followed by the third finger, in the rhythm of a triplet. Practice making the attack of the left hand sound similar to the attack of the right hand.

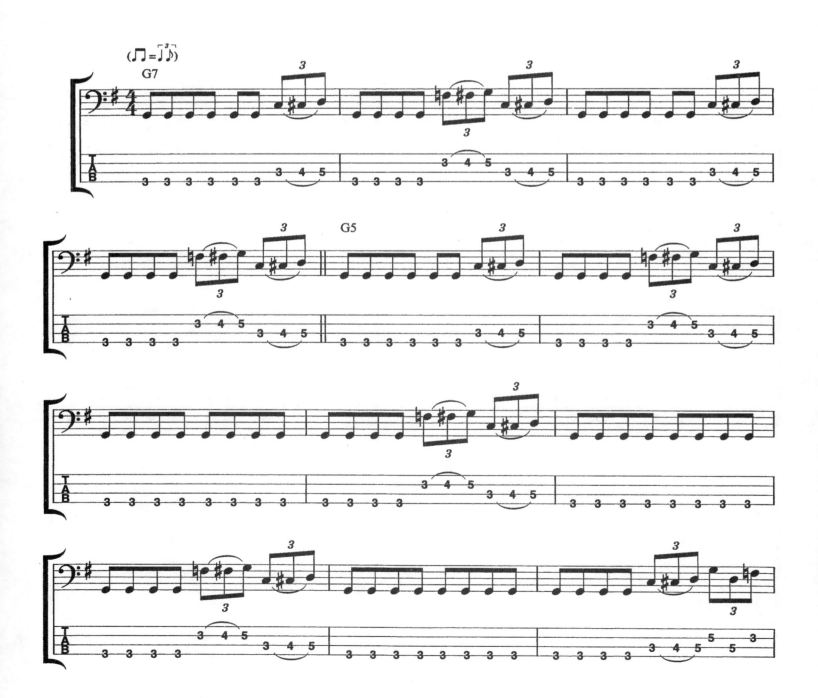

Example 81

This example is in the style known as the **Chicago shuffle**. The Chicago shuffle is characterized by its root down to the fifth movement, alternating shuffle eighth notes root–fifth (C–G). The example also uses connecting lines similar to those used in previous examples.

Example 82

This example introduces the **boogie feel**. A boogie feel is a shuffle characterized by a constantly repeated bass figure, which is highly syncopated and stresses the up-beats over the down-beats. This feel is important to learn, due to the fact that rock music has been greatly influenced by boogie music. The important thing to remember about the boogie feel is that it is extremely syncopated, with most of the notes occurring on the up-beats.

Example 83

This example is similar to Example 81 only this time using **power chords**. A power chord is played by combining the root and the fifth together, and is similar to playing a major or minor triad without the third. This makes the power chord very popular in rock and blues because when improvising, both thirds can be used without clashing with the chords.

E power chord:

Example 84

This example is a boogie feel in 12/8, meaning there are 12 eighth notes per measure. This is similar to playing triplets in 4/4 time, much like a shuffle feel. The feel is set up by alternating the right hand fingers on the third and fourth strings. Remember to keep your right hand fingers in the same position and you will get a consistent sound.

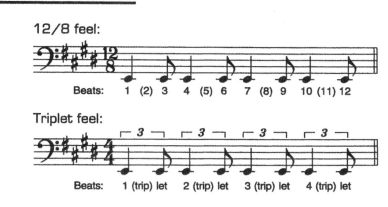

Example 85

This example is the primary riff from the tune "Lies" by Tim Bogart. Like Example 84, this example is in 12/8 and the triplet feel is set up by the right hand. The example alternates between the open fourth string root (E) and the 6 (C#), flat 7 (D) and octave on the third string, and ends with a very common descending minor pentatonic riff.

Example 86

This example uses a major pentatonic pattern similar to Example 75, but this time uses shuffle eighth notes instead of straight eighth notes.

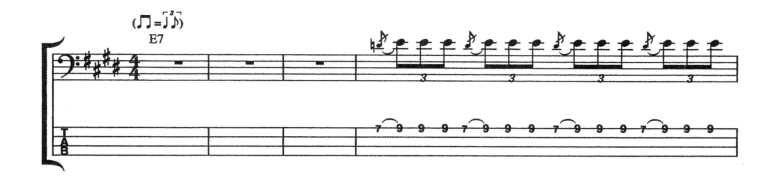

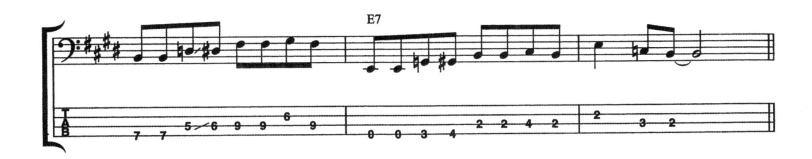

120

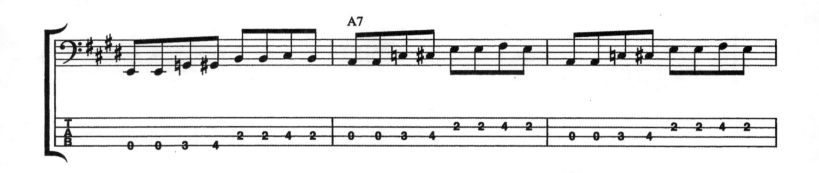

TAPPING, HARMONICS AND DOUBLE-STOPS

This section will cover some "tricky little bits" that work really well to impress people: tapping, harmonics and double-stops. **Tapping** is a fun thing, made popular by Billy Sheehan. While holding your left hand finger on the neck, you "tap" the note to the fretboard with the tip of your right hand index finger, then pull down on the string as you release the right hand note to sound the left hand note.

Example 87

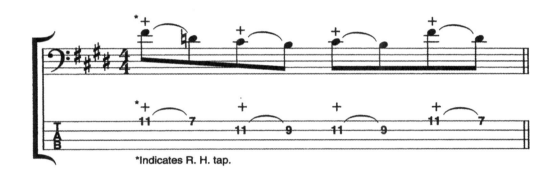

*Indicates R. H. tap.

Tapping can also be used in conjunction with left hand hammer-ons and pull-offs.

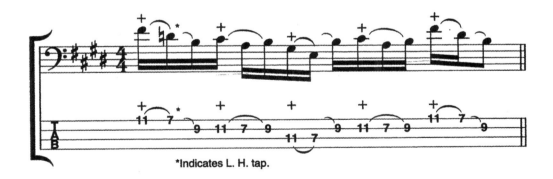

*Indicates L. H. tap.

122

Example 88

Harmonics are found at various points on the bass and
can be used to play chords, melodies or just for effect. To
play a harmonic on the bass, lightly touch the string
directly over a fret (do not depress the string to the fretboard). Pluck with the picking hand. You should hear a
ringing "bell" like sound.

By combining more than one harmonic, they can be
used to play chords. If you play the harmonics at the
fifth fret on the first and second strings with the open
fourth string, they combine to form a lovely E minor 7
chord.

Practice locating the various harmonics on the bass and experiment with using them in scales
and chords.

Example 89

Double-stops are simply playing two notes at the same time. A common technique is to
harmonize a scale using double-stops in a series of major and minor thirds, using the notes
from that scale.

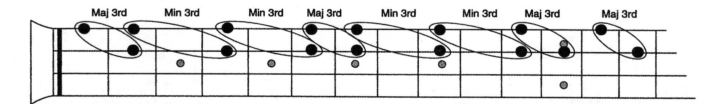

The example below shows the E mixolydian scale (which is the same as the A major scale
starting on E) harmonized up to the octave, all played on the first two strings. After reaching
the octave, the pattern repeats again (as far as the neck on your bass allows).

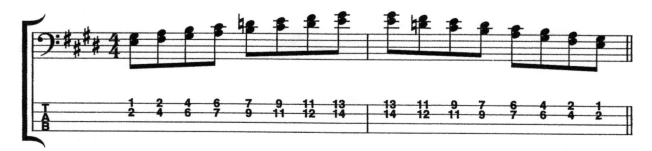

Example 90

This example combines two of the previous techniques into one exercise. It begins with the harmonics at the fifth and seventh frets, and then moves into the tapping section. Remember to start slowly and gradually increase the tempo using a metronome or drum machine.

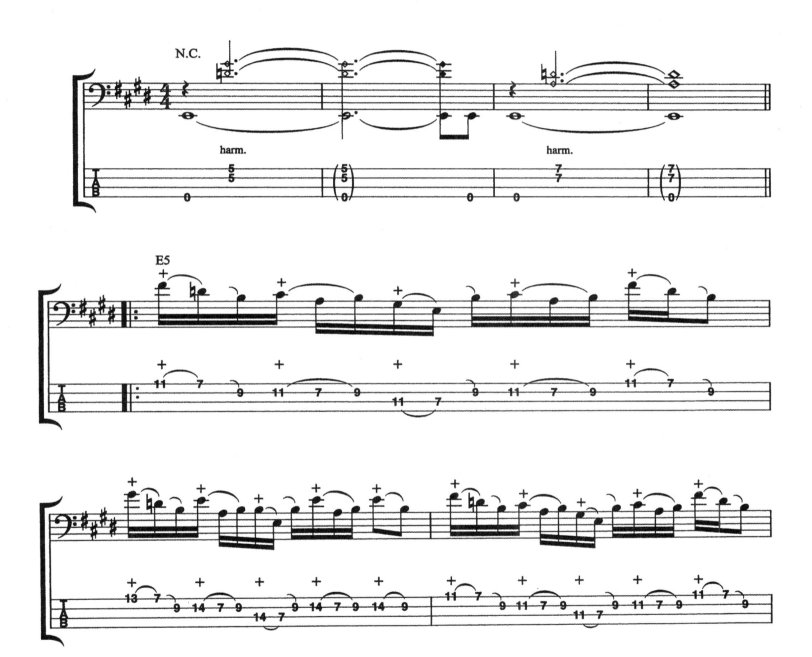

124

Example 91

This exercise introduces a technique known as a "power slide," which is simply playing the fifth fret D power chord and sliding it up to the seventh fret E power chord. The example also uses the slash chord, where the third is used in the bass instead of the root.

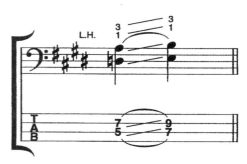

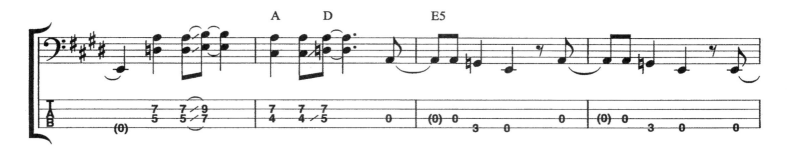

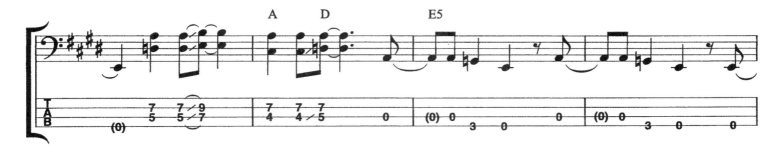

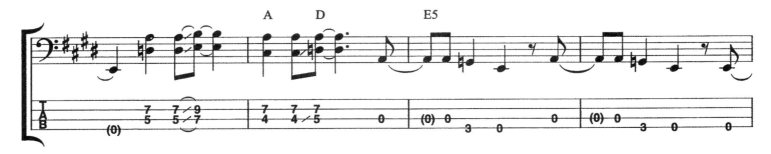

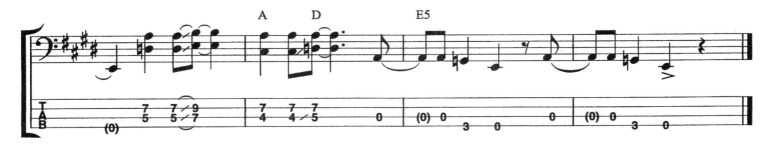

BASS FINGERBOARD CHART

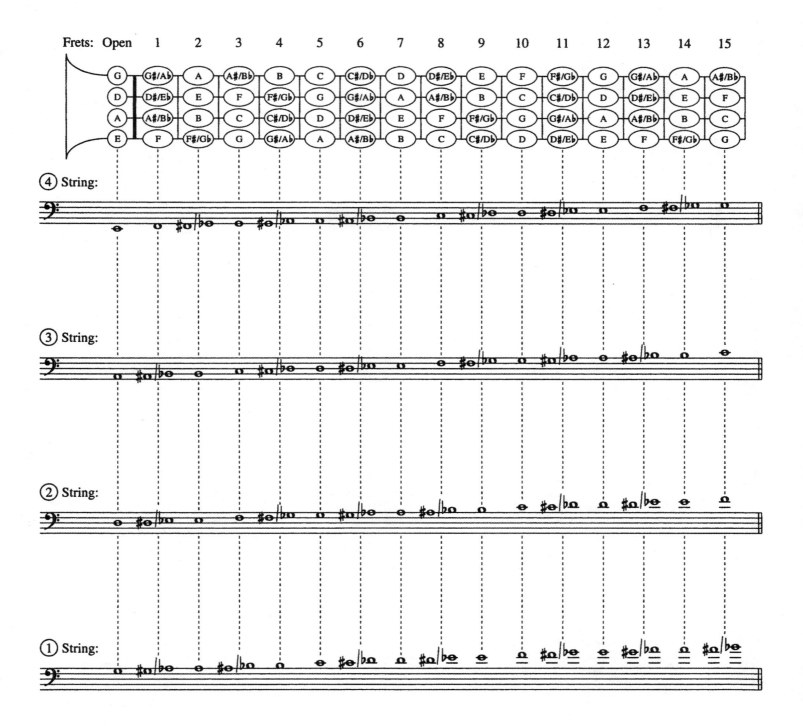